3rd Grade Workbooks:
Printing Practice
for Kids

SPEEDY
PUBLISHING

Speedy Publishing LLC
40 E. Main St. #1156
Newark, DE 19711
www.speedypublishing.com

My ambition is...

I love to...

My favorite pet...

My mother...

My father...

_____
_____
_____
_____
_____
_____
_____
_____
_____
_____
_____

My family...

My bestfriend...

My favorite color...

My favorite food..

My favorite teacher..

My favorite subject...

My hobbies are...

_____

_____

_____

_____

_____

_____

_____

_____

_____

_____

I am named.. because..

I love Monday..

I love Friday...

I love Saturday..

_____

_____

_____

_____

_____

_____

_____

_____

_____

_____

I love Sunday..

My favorite show..

My favorite character...

_____

_____

_____

_____

_____

_____

_____

_____

_____

_____

_____

My idol..

My favorite hero...

My favorite game...

I want...

_____

_____

_____

_____

_____

_____

_____

_____

_____

_____

I am happy when...

I would like to go to...

If I have a superpower...

If I could fly...

My favorite movie...

During Christmas...

_____

_____

_____

_____

_____

_____

_____

_____

_____

_____

50569844R10020

Made in the USA
Columbia, SC
08 February 2019